CONTENTS

Some words are printed in bold, **like this.** You can find out what they mean by looking in the glossary.

DEEP, DARK, AND DANGEROUS

Under the surface of the sea lies a hidden and strange world. This place is home to hundreds of thousands of kinds of creatures. Many of these creatures have never even been seen by humans.

Scientists think there may be around one million unknown **species** of animals in the deep sea.

Creatures of the Deep

EXTRAORDINARY EELS

Casey Rand

Raintree

www.raintreepublishers.co.uk
Visit our website to find out
more information about
Raintree books.

To order:
☎ Phone 0845 6044371
🖹 Fax +44 (0) 1865 312263
🖥 Email myorders@raintreepublishers.co.uk

Customers from outside the UK please telephone +44 1865 312262

Raintree is an imprint of Capstone Global Library Limited,
a company incorporated in England and Wales having its
registered office at 7 Pilgrim Street, London, EC4V 6LB –
Registered company number: 6695582

Edited by Megan Cotugno and Abby Colich
Designed by Philippa Jenkins
Picture research by Hannah Taylor
Illustrated by Terry Pastor / www.theartagency.co.uk
Originated by Capstone Global Library
Printed and bound in China by CTPS

ISBN 978 1 406 22639 3 (hardback)
15 14 13 12 11
10 9 8 7 6 5 4 3 2 1

ISBN 978 1 406 22646 1 (paperback)
16 15 14 13 12
10 9 8 7 6 5 4 3 2 1

British Library Cataloguing in Publication Data
Rand, Casey.
Extraordinary eels. -- (Creatures of the deep)
597.4'3-dc22
A full catalogue record for this book is available from the
British Library.

Acknowledgements
We would like to thank the following for permission to
reproduce photographs: Corbis p. **19** (Sam Forencich); FLPA
pp. **5** (Richard Herrmann/Minden Pictures), **8** (Fred
Bavendam/Minden Pictures), **10** (Reinhard Dirscherl), **13**
(Norbert Wu/Minden Pictures), **17** (David Hosking), **18**
(D P Wilson), **28** (Wil Meinderts/FN/Minden); Getty Images
pp. **26** (US Coast Guard), **27** (AFP/Mark Ralston); Image
Quest Marine pp. **14** (Hal Beral), **20** (Dray van Beeck), **25**
(Andre Seale); naturepl.com pp. **4, 7** (David Shale), **24**
(Sinclair Stummers); Photolibrary pp. **9, 12** (Waterframe
Images/Rodger Klein), **11, 15, 21** (Oxford Scientific/David B
Fleetham), **22** (Peter Arnold Images/Nicole Duplaix), **23**
(Oxford Scientific/Fitor Angel).

Cover photograph of a Giant moray eel (*gymnothorax
javanicus*) in the Red Sea reproduced with permission of
naturepl.com (Jeff Rotman).

We would like to thank Michael Bright for his invaluable help
in the preparation of this book.

Every effort has been made to contact copyright holders
of material reproduced in this book. Any omissions will
be rectified in subsequent printings if notice is given to
the publisher.

Scientists must use special types of ships called **submersibles** to explore the deep sea.

Deep

The deepest part of the ocean is more than 11,000 metres (36,000 feet) deep. That is about 11 kilometres (7 miles) straight down! What unknown creatures lurk this far below the surface?

Dark

Sunlight can usually only pass through to around 200 metres (656 feet) of water. From this depth all the way to the floor of the ocean, there is complete darkness. How can creatures see through this darkness?

Dangerous

In the deep sea, the water is extremely cold. Oxygen levels are low, and **pressure** from the water above is enormous. It is very dangerous. How do scientists explore these areas?

CREATURES OF THE DEEP

Animals that live in the depths of the deep sea have special features that help them deal with the darkness and dangers of their **habitat**.

Scientists have divided the ocean, from surface to floor, into five zones.

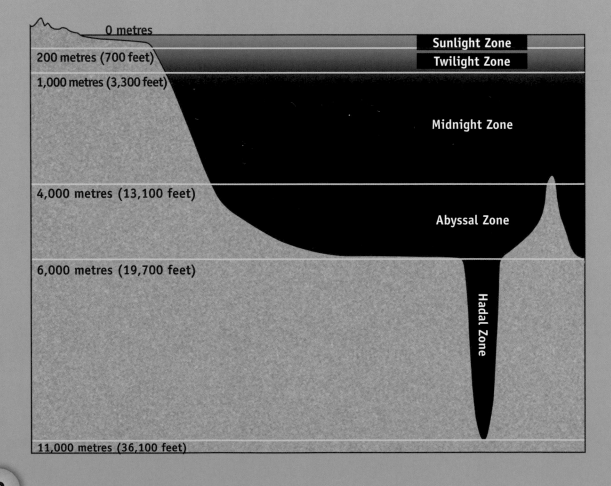

0 metres

200 metres (700 feet)

1,000 metres (3,300 feet)

4,000 metres (13,100 feet)

6,000 metres (19,700 feet)

11,000 metres (36,100 feet)

Sunlight Zone

Twilight Zone

Midnight Zone

Abyssal Zone

Hadal Zone

Most eels live in the sunlight and twilight zones, but the snipe eel has been found as deep as 1,800 metres (6,000 feet).

The eel

In all of the waters of the world, there are more than 790 **species** of eels. There are both freshwater and saltwater eels. Most prefer to live in shallow waters, but there are many amazing and mysterious deep-sea eels, too.

Fit for sea

The body of the eel is built to survive the deep sea. Eel bodies are made of both small bones and **cartilage**, like the material in your ear. Cartilage is very flexible and will not be crushed by the **pressure** of the sea.

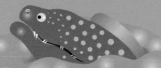

THE GIANT BELOW

One of the most amazing ocean eels is the giant moray eel. This is the world's largest eel. It can reach up to 3 metres (10 feet) in length and weigh 29 kilograms (65 pounds).

Cave dweller

Moray eels prefer to live mainly on coral reefs. They also hide in holes or crevices in the reef wall at depths of a few hundred metres. These holes and caves in which eels live are called **eel pits**.

The giant moray hides in an eel pit.

This dwarf moray eel is closely related to the giant moray but is only a few inches long.

Creatures great and small

The smallest of the moray eels is the Snyder's moray. This tiny moray only grows to about 11.5 centimetres (4.5 inches) long.

Moray family

The moray family of eels has more than 80 **species** of eels, including the giant moray. There is great variety in the size, colour, and behaviour of eels in the moray family.

MEET THE MORAY EEL

Many scuba divers have come across the giant moray eel with its razor sharp teeth. It can be a terrifying experience. But the giant moray does not usually attack humans unless it is threatened.

Snake of the water

The giant moray swims by slithering through the water, a bit like the motion a snake makes while moving on land. Because of this snake-like movement they use, the moray can swim forwards and backwards!

The moray eel slithers through the water.

A large mouth helps the moray eel filter oxygen from the water so it can breathe.

Open wide

The giant moray eel is usually seen with its mouth wide open, showing its sharp teeth. This is not because the eel is about to bite. Moray eels open wide to suck water into their mouths. They then filter oxygen from the water. This is how a moray eel breathes.

Tiny eyes

The moray eel has very small eyes and very poor eyesight. Scientists believe the eyes of most moray eels are used only to detect light.

RIBBON AND GULPER EELS

The brilliantly coloured ribbon eel is another member of the moray eel family. Amazingly, male and female ribbon eels look almost nothing alike in their colouring. The male is bright blue with yellow fins and face. The female has a yellow body and head with black fins.

Gulper eel

The gulper eel is a bit scary to look at. It has a huge mouth that can be used to swallow prey even larger than itself. The gulper is not actually part of the eel family, but is called a "gulper eel" because it looks very similar to some types of eel.

Like other moray eels, the ribbon eel often hides in **eel pits**.

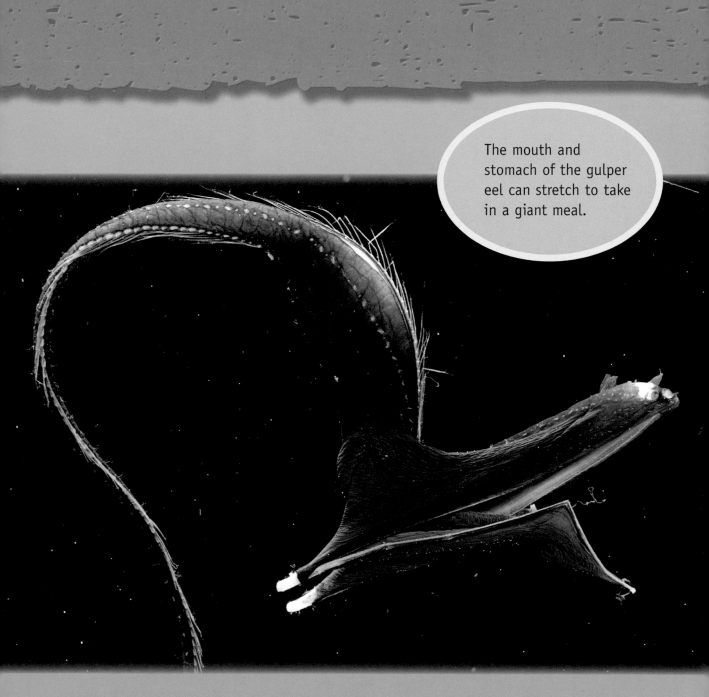

The mouth and stomach of the gulper eel can stretch to take in a giant meal.

Gone fishing

The gulper eel has a special organ at the end of its tail that allows it to glow and flash light. This organ is known as **photophore**. It is used as a fishing lure to attract fish for the gulper to eat.

HUNTERS AND HUNTED

Eels are **carnivores**. This means that eels are meat eaters. Most eels eat fish, clams, squid, and even other eels. Eels prefer to hunt at night. Although eels have poor eyesight, they have a very good sense of smell. They usually wait in holes or crevices for something they want to eat to wander close enough. The eel then shoots out of the hole and grabs its meal.

Eels are skilled hunters.

The barracuda is a powerful predator of the eel.

Hunted

Eels are hunted by many other sea creatures, including the barracuda. The barracuda is a large **predator** with razor-sharp, fang-like teeth. They can swim up to 43 kilometres per hour (27 miles per hour) when they are chasing an eel or other **prey**. Some types of eel are eaten by humans as well, but their blood can be poisonous if not cooked correctly.

ALIEN JAWS

Some eels have a unique feature. They have two sets of jaws. The moray eel has one set of large, sharp teeth in the front of its mouth. It uses these to grab and hold its **prey**. The moray also has a second set of jaws that thrust forwards from its throat. This set of jaws pulls the food down into the eel's stomach.

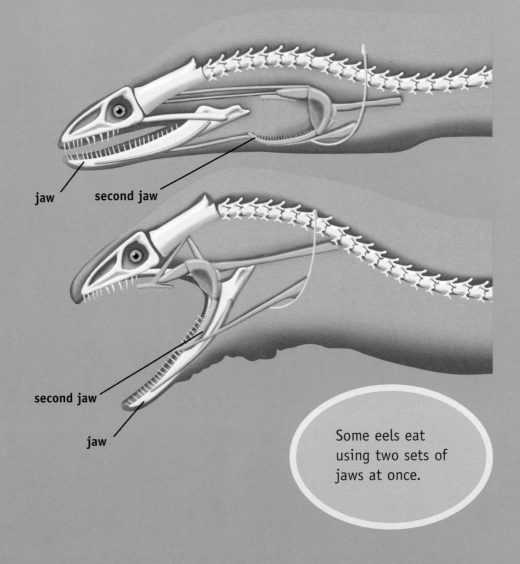

jaw

second jaw

second jaw

jaw

Some eels eat using two sets of jaws at once.

Death roll

Alligators are famous for clamping down on their prey and then spinning quickly around several times to tear meat from their prey. This is known as a death roll. Some eels use a similar strategy when they capture prey too large to eat in one bite.

Alligators and eels have similar strategies for hunting large prey.

Tied up in knots

The eel can use its long, slender body to get into a good position for capturing and eating prey. They can also knot themselves as a way to escape capture.

MONSTER EELS

While the giant moray eel can look very scary, there are other types of eel that may be even more frightening. In fact, one of these eels may even be mistaken for a very famous monster.

Conger eel

The conger eel is a monstrous kind of eel. It can grow up to 3 metres (10 feet) in length and weigh more than 45 kilograms (100 pounds). It has extremely sharp teeth and a powerful jaw. These eels will eat almost anything they can catch.

The monstrous conger eel is a fierce hunter.

Could the Loch Ness Monster be a giant conger eel?

The Loch Ness Monster

In Loch Ness, in Scotland, some people believe a monster is roaming the waters. This monster has become famously known as the Loch Ness Monster. This monster may only be a **myth**, or made up story. Some people believe the Loch Ness Monster could be a very large eel that people mistake for a monster. But some pictures show the Loch Ness Monster raising its head out of the water. Eels are not known to do this.

TIGERS, SNAKES, AND DRAGONS

There are many interesting and unique eels in the sea. Some eels even look a little bit like animals from outside the sea.

Swimming tiger

The tiger snake eel looks like a poisonous sea snake. These eels live in tropical and warm water areas. They can grow up to about 1 metre (40 inches) long. These eels are known for their ability to dig a small hole with their tails and burrow in.

The tiger snake eel normally lives buried in the ground, but will come out to feed.

The brilliantly coloured dragon eel is a ferocious predator.

Mimicry

The eel's ability to mimic, or look like, a poisonous snake is known as **mimicry**. Mimicry helps the eel to scare off **predators** by making the predator think it is a harmful animal.

Dragon eel

The dragon eel is a unique looking eel. It has many bright colours and two horns that grow out from the top of its head. The dragon eel is very aggressive with razor-sharp teeth. It will eat anything it can catch.

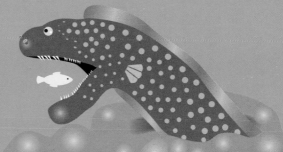

ELECTRIFYING EELS

Zap! The electric eel produces its own electricity, just like a battery. It has been known to zap a few unsuspecting victims who accidentally step on it.

Stunned

The electric eel can produce a shock up to five times as powerful as the shock from an electrical socket! Eels mainly use electric shocks to stun their **prey**, or to help them escape **predators**. They also use weaker electric signals to communicate with other eels.

These eels have a shocking hunting strategy.

The electric eel is not the only fish that can produce electricity. This electric ray can have the same shocking effect.

Shocking

Electric eels are not actually part of the eel family. They are more closely related to the catfish than to the moray family of eels.

	Eel family	Electric eel
Water	Fresh and salt	Fresh only
Teeth	Has teeth	Does not have teeth
Breathe	Underwater	Air breathers

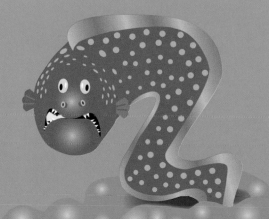

FROM EGG TO EEL

Eels normally live anywhere from 10 to 30 years. During this time, they grow and change just like humans grow and change as they get older.

Catching the current

A mother eel may lay millions of eggs at once. When these eggs begin to hatch, the baby eels float to the surface and begin to drift in the ocean **current**. The eels will continue drifting along for six months to one year. Eels may travel halfway around the world just floating in the ocean currents.

Baby eels are flat and **transparent**. This helps them remain hidden as they grow.

Adult eels usually die after **reproducing**.

Growing up

As the eels get older, they start to look like adult eels. They will eventually be ready to find a mate. Many eels travel and remain alone their entire lives until it is time to mate. At this time, eels will travel together to a safe place for laying eggs.

CATASTROPHE AT SEA

In 2010 an oil well in the Gulf of Mexico was damaged from an explosion, and oil began spilling into the sea. This oil spill has already cost billions of dollars to clean up, but even more disastrous is the massive effect it will have on sea life.

Toxic spill

Oil does not mix well with water, so spilled oil floats on the water's surface. Floating oil attracts many types of sea animals, as they think it may be food. However, oil is known to be **toxic**, or poisonous, to almost all forms of life. It is especially dangerous for baby animals and eggs.

Massive efforts are made to stop oil leaks.

Floating oil can be extremely dangerous to sea life.

Eels and oil

While deep-sea eels may not come into contact with this toxic floating oil, **plumes** of oil deep underwater may harm them. Many of the fish, shrimp, and other animals that eels hunt are harmed by oil spills. This could cause a dangerous shortage of food for deep-sea eels and other deep-sea animals.

DANGER IN THE WATER

Some eels are considered highly endangered, or at risk of becoming **extinct**. Dams and power plants built on rivers can cause danger to the ability of eels to **migrate** and **reproduce**. Other eels are in danger because they are fished too heavily for human food.

Poison

The giant moray and many other morays are not considered endangered. This may be partly because they are poisonous to humans, and therefore are not fished heavily. However the American and European eels are heavily fished and are already at risk in some areas.

Many eels, like this European eel, are becoming endangered.

Save the eel

Scientists are developing ways to make sure the eel is not in danger of extinction. One plan is developing a **sonar system**, like that used in submarines, to detect approaching eels. When the sonar system detects an eel, it would shut down the power plants to allow eels to pass by more easily.

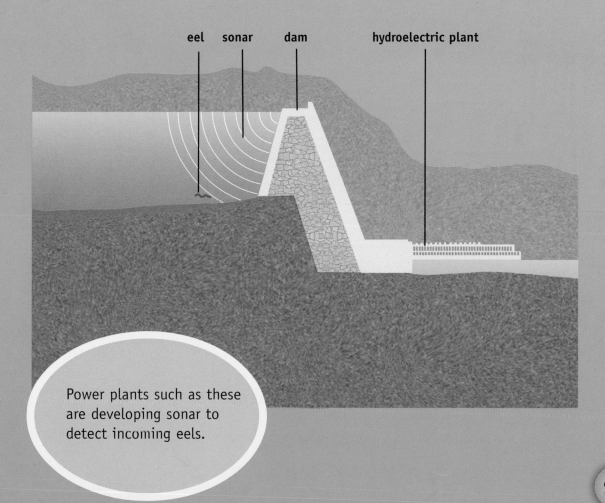

eel   sonar   dam   hydroelectric plant

Power plants such as these are developing sonar to detect incoming eels.

GLOSSARY

carnivore meat-eating creature

cartilage elastic connective tissue found in various parts of the body, such as the joints

current movement of ocean water

eel pit small hole, cave, or crevice in which eels live

extinct when an organism no longer exists

habitat place where a plant or animal lives

migrate move from one place to another

mimicry similarity between two different species that protects one or both of the species from predators

myth false story that many have come to believe as true

photophore light-producing organ found especially in marine fish

plume column or band of a substance

predator organism that lives by hunting other organisms for food

pressure weight or force that pushes against something

prey animal that is hunted by other animals

reproduce have babies

sonar system method in which some types of machine and some animals use sound waved to detect objects

species specific group of animals that share a name and traits and are able to interbreed

submersible small underwater craft

toxic poisonous

transparent lacking colour and able to be seen through

FIND OUT MORE

Books

Steve Backshall's Deadly 60, Stephen Backshall
   (New Holland Publishers, 2009)

*Life in the Crusher: Mysteries of the Deep Oceans
   (Extreme!)*, Trevor Day (A & C Black, 2009)

Ecosystems (Planet Earth), Jim Pipe (TickTock
   Books, 2008)

Websites

**ngkids.co.uk/cool_stories/1258/myths__monsters_
   and_marvels_of_the_deep**
Read about the scary stories inspired by the mysteries
of the ocean.

www.nessie.co.uk/index.html
Find out more about the legend of the Loch Ness
Monster, including sightings and expeditions.

www.deepseaconservation.org/index.php
Visit this website to find out more about the deep
waters of the United Kingdom and how we can help to
protect them.

INDEX